BIBLE EXPLORERS

Jesus Does Amazing Things!

Leena Lane - Gillian Chapman

The wedding at Cana

Jesus was invited to a wedding at Cana in Galilee.

There was a great feast and everyone was enjoying the party. Then suddenly the wine began to run out.

'Do something to help,' said Mary, Jesus' mother.

Jesus knew what God wanted him to do. He told the servant to fill six large stone jars with water, then take them to the man in charge of the feast.

When the man tasted it, he was very pleased.

'Wonderful!' said the man. 'People usually serve the best wine first, but you have left the best wine till last!'

He didn't know that Jesus had worked a miracle. Jesus had turned the water into wine!

John 2, verses 1 to 10

Something to think about:

Jesus can do amazing things if we ask him.

Prayer:

Dear God, thank you that you can make ordinary things special.

Activity:

How many jar handles can you see?

How many stone jars with the same red zig-zag pattern can you find?

A man with leprosy

Jesus went with his friends to a nearby town. They met a man there who had a terrible skin disease called leprosy. Nobody went near the man. He was very lonely and in pain. He hoped that Jesus could help him.

When the man saw Jesus coming, he threw himself at Jesus' feet, crying, 'Lord, you can make me well again, if you want to.'

Jesus put his hand on the man and said, 'Yes, I do want to make you well. You are healed!'

All at once, the man's skin became normal and he was completely well again!

Jesus told him not to tell anyone about it, but to go to the priest.

'Show him that you are well again,' said Jesus, 'and offer a gift to God. Everyone will know that God has healed you.'

News about what Jesus had done spread throughout the town.

Luke 5, verses 12 to 16

Something to think about:

Jesus asked the man to give a gift to God for making him well again. Do we remember to thank God when he answers our prayers?

Prayer:

Dear God,
help me to care about people who are ill. Help me to remember to ask you to help them.

Activity:

Can you see ten differences between the two pictures?

The soldier's servant

One day, a Roman officer came to Jesus for help.

'My servant is very ill,' he said. 'He is too ill to leave the house.'

Jesus replied, 'Then I will go to your house and make him well.'

'No, no,' said the officer. 'I know how busy you are. But if you just say the word, I know he will be healed.'

Jesus was surprised to hear this. He was pleased to find that the officer trusted him.

'Go home, then,' said Jesus. 'What you believe will be done.'

The officer ran home. He found to his great joy that his servant had been made well again!

Luke 7, verses 1 to 10

Something to think about:

Is Jesus ever too busy to listen to us?

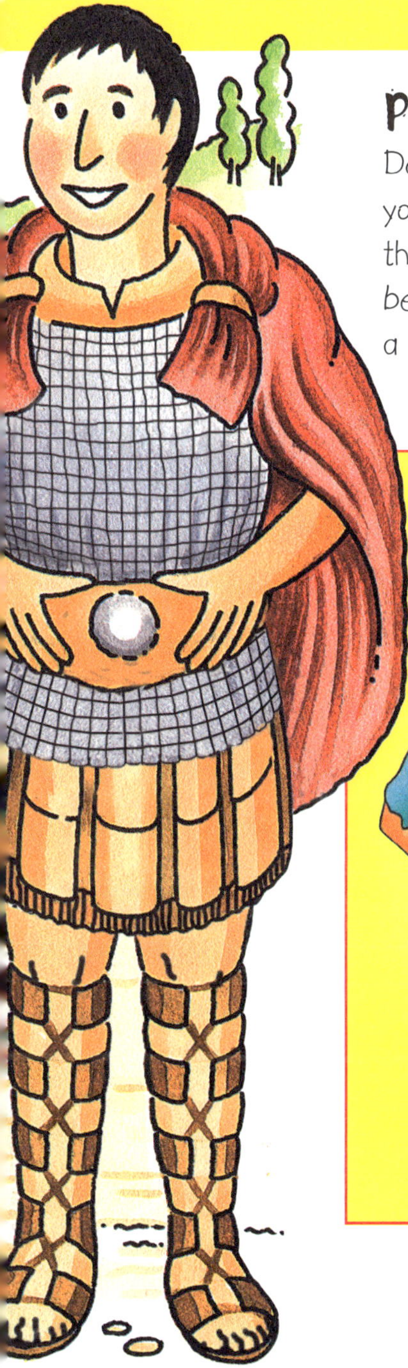

Prayer:

Dear God, help me to tell you about all the things that worry me, and then believe that you can make a difference.

Activity:

One of these soldiers is shown here with Jesus. Tick the box to show which one it is.

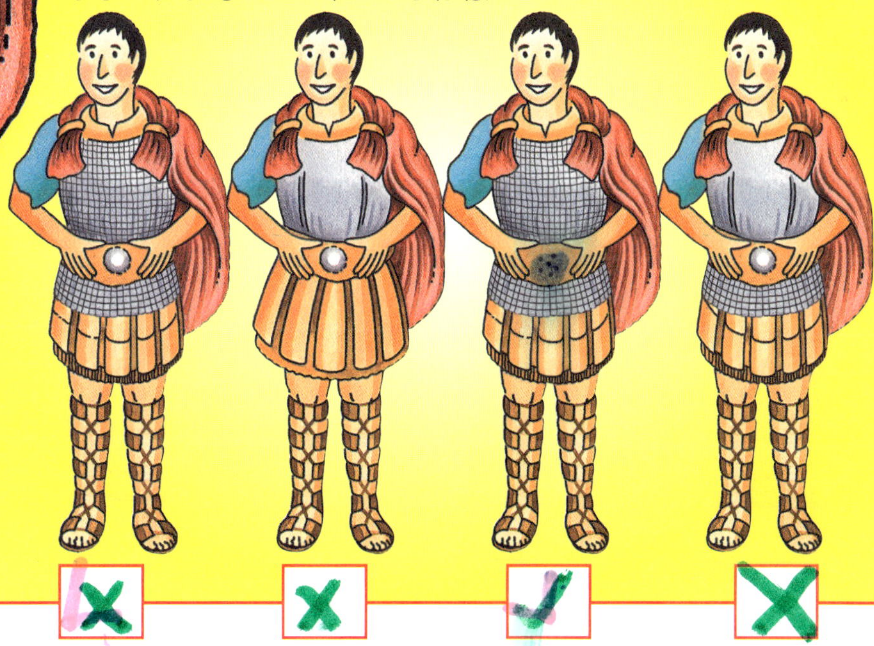

Jesus helps a man to walk again

One day Jesus was speaking to a group of teachers of the Law, when some unexpected visitors arrived...

Jesus was inside a house talking to the teachers. There was a rustling noise above them and suddenly a large hole appeared in the ceiling!

Faces peered through the hole, and a mat was lowered down. On the mat lay a man who could not walk. His friends knew that Jesus could heal him. They could not bring him through the door because of all the crowds, so they had taken him up the stairs outside. They had thought of another way of getting in – by making a hole in the roof!

Jesus looked at the man kindly and said, 'Your sins are forgiven.'

The teachers grumbled – who did Jesus think he was? God himself?

Then Jesus said to the man, 'Stand up! Pick up your mat and walk.'

At once the man stood up and walked home, praising God for the amazing miracle which had happened.

Luke 5, verses 17 to 26

Something to think about:

The man's friends thought of an unusual way to reach Jesus. Can we help our friends to find him too?

Prayer:

Dear God, thank you for the friends who help us. Help me to be a special friend to people around me.

Activity:

These ropes are all tangled up. Can you tell how many ropes there are?

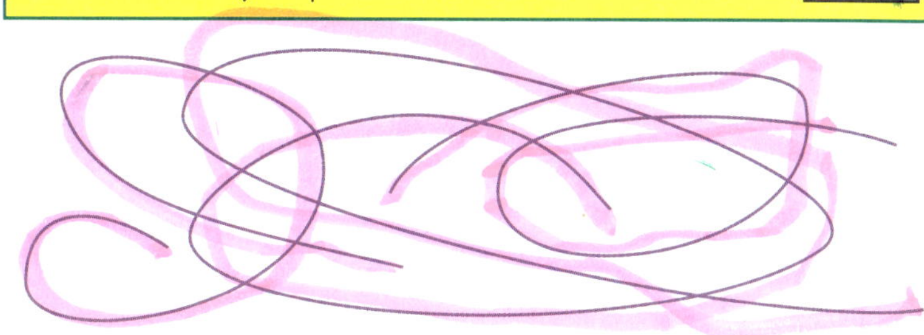

Activity:

Can you unscramble these words to find what the house roof was made of?

_ _ a _ _ _ _ s AND _ _ _

n a s h c r e b   m d u

Jesus makes a blind man see

One day people brought a blind man to Jesus. They wanted Jesus to make him see again.

Jesus walked with him out of the village. Then Jesus spat on the man's eyes and gently put his hands on them.

'Can you see anything yet?' asked Jesus.

'I can see some people, but they are all fuzzy, like trees walking around.'

So Jesus put his hands on the man's eyes a second time. This time the man opened his eyes and could see perfectly! He was amazed to see the colourful world and the kind face of Jesus.

'Go home now,' said Jesus, 'but don't go back to the village.'

Mark 8, verses 22 to 26

Something to think about:

Hold your hands over your eyes and imagine being blind. Now lift them off and imagine how the blind man felt when he could see again.

Prayer:

Dear God, thank you that you can change people's lives.

Activity:

Can you see what each of these silhouettes is?

Jesus calms a storm

One day, Jesus and his friends got into a boat on the lake. It had been a very busy day and Jesus was tired.

Suddenly a fierce storm blew up. The boat was rocked about like a cork, and the waves splashed over the side. The disciples were terrified of sinking. But Jesus was fast asleep.

'Save us, Lord!' they shouted to Jesus.

'Why are you so afraid?' said Jesus, waking up.

Then Jesus got up and ordered the wind and the waves to calm down.

The storm vanished. Everyone was amazed!

'Even the wind and the waves obey him!' they said.

Jesus had saved his friends from drowning in the storm.

Luke 8, verses 22 to 25

Something to think about:

Jesus' friends were with him all the time, but even they didn't understand that he had power over the natural world.

Prayer:

Help me to talk to you when I am afraid, Lord God. Please be there to take away my fears.

Activity:

Find two words below that describe each of the following:

- ☐ ☐ Jesus
- ☐ ☐ The weather
- ☐ ☐ The disciples

Q	W	I	C	D	Y	F	C	T
W	S	T	O	R	M	Y	W	I
A	S	L	E	E	P	M	I	R
R	Y	R	N	W	Z	F	N	E
S	B	A	M	A	Z	E	D	D
Y	D	D	J	Y	E	K	Y	U
T	E	R	R	I	F	I	E	D
M	R	T	A	J	S	O	N	P
A	E	S	G	H	I	O	P	B

Jesus feeds a hungry crowd

Jesus was once speaking to a large crowd of people. There were men, women and even children. They had been listening to him all day and were getting hungry.

Jesus' friends thought the people should go away and buy some food, but Jesus wanted to feed them.

'Where can we buy food for all these people?' he asked his friends.

Philip replied, 'We would need more than two hundred silver coins to buy enough!'

Andrew, another of Jesus' friends, said, 'There is a boy who says he will share his lunch. But he has only five rolls and two small fishes.'

But then Jesus did something amazing! He thanked God for the food, then shared it out amongst everyone!

No one went away hungry. Jesus gave them all enough to eat, and there were even twelve baskets full of left-overs.

John 6, verses 1 to 13

Something to think about:

Jesus accepts even the small amount we offer him and does great things with it.

Prayer:

Help me, Lord God, to share all that I have with those around me.

Activity:

After everyone had eaten, there were still many *baskets* of food left over. How many *baskets* can you count?

Jesus walks on the water

After Jesus had fed the crowds, his friends went down to the lake where they found a boat. They set off across the lake for Capernaum. Jesus was not with them.

A stormy wind blew up and the water on the lake became choppy. The men kept on rowing, but were rather scared.

Suddenly they saw Jesus coming towards them. He was walking on the water! They couldn't believe what they saw and were very afraid.

'Don't be frightened,' said Jesus. 'You all know me – your friend, Jesus.'

They wanted him to come aboard. At once the boat reached the shore and they were all safe.

John 6, verses 16 to 21

Something to think about:
How could Jesus walk on the water?

Prayer:

Dear God, help us to remember that Jesus can do more than we can ever imagine.

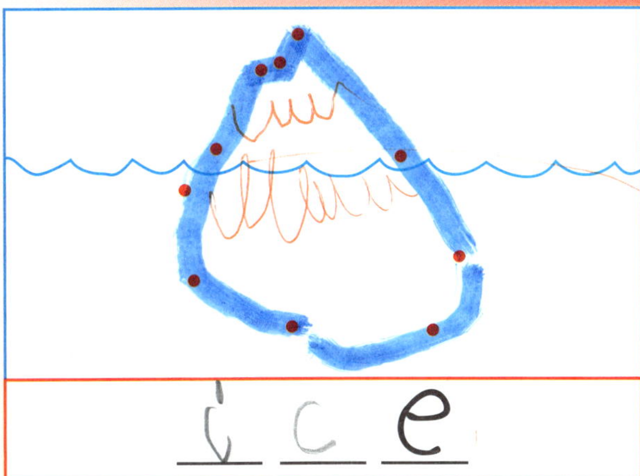

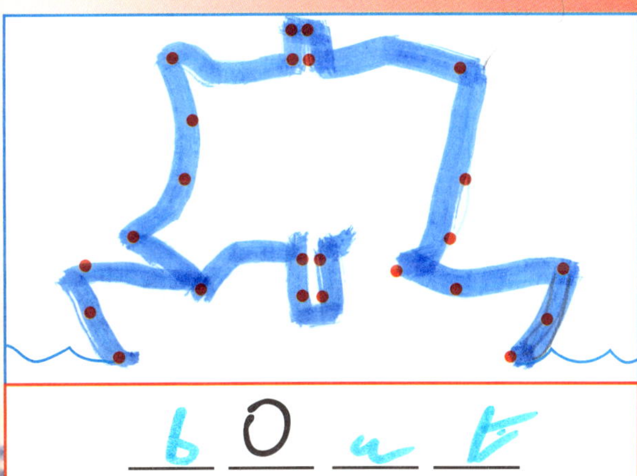

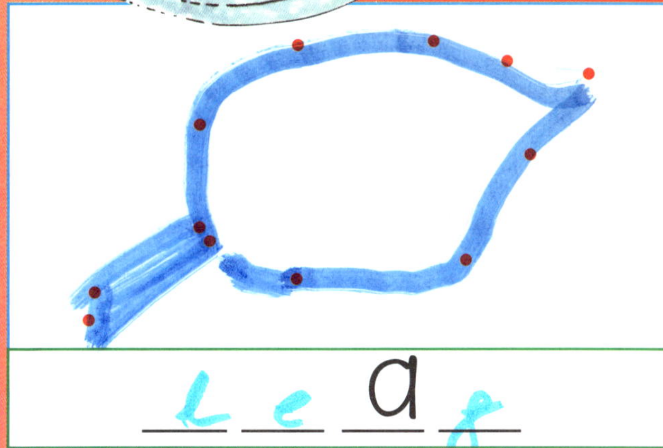

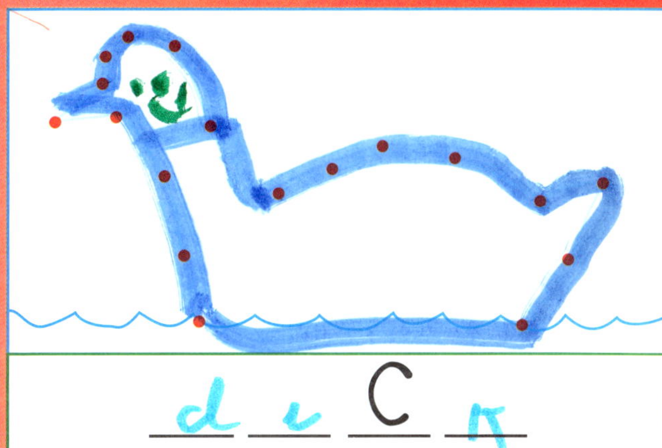

Activity:

Lots of things can float on water, but only Jesus could walk on water. Can you join the dots to complete the pictures and name the things that float on water?

Jesus heals Jairus' daughter

One day Jesus was asked to help a man called Jairus whose daughter was dying. Was there anything Jesus could do? Jairus loved his daughter so much. If only Jesus could reach her in time...

But there were huge crowds around Jesus and a woman came forward to touch Jesus' cloak. She had been ill for years, and Jesus healed her. It was a wonderful day for her.

Suddenly a messenger from Jairus' house came with some dreadful news. Jairus' daughter was dead.

'Don't be afraid,' said Jesus. 'Believe, and she will be healed.'

They hurried to Jairus' house and Jesus saw the girl who was dead. Everyone was weeping and wailing with sadness.

Jesus held the girl's hand and said, 'Get up, my child!'

The girl came back to life and stood up!

'Give her some food,' said Jesus to her parents. 'She's hungry.'

They were amazed at what Jesus had done, and overjoyed to have their little girl back again.

Luke 8, verses 40 to 56

Prayer:

Dear God, help me to keep on trusting you when I find something difficult. Thank you that you hear my prayers.

Activity: Colour in this picture.

Something to think about:

Everyone had given up hope that Jairus' daughter would be saved. But Jesus came to the rescue!

The healing at the pool

There was a pool in Jerusalem called Bethesda. Many people who couldn't walk or see used to lie there, hoping to be healed when the water in the pool was stirred up.

Jesus came to the pool and saw a man who had been unable to walk for thirty-eight years.

'Do you want to get well?' Jesus asked him.

'I have no one to help me into the pool,' replied the man. 'Someone else always gets there first.'

Jesus said to the man, 'Get up! Pick up your mat and walk!'

The water hadn't

stirred in the pool. But Jesus had healed the man. He could walk again!

John 5, verses 1 to 9

Activity:

Can you answer these questions about other people that Jesus healed?
Write the answers in the boxes provided.

This man described people as fuzzy what?

walking trees

Whose daughter is this?

Jinis

What did Jesus ask her parents to give her?

food

What did this man suffer from?

leprosy

What did this disease affect?

Skin

This man entered the room through ...?

the roof

Jesus said, 'Pick up your mat and ... .'?

go home

Prayer:

Dear God, thank you that Jesus did amazing miracles and can still help people today.

Something to think about:

What do you think you'd do first if you could walk again after thirty-eight years?

The amazing catch of fish

After Jesus was crucified, God raised Jesus from the dead. The stone was rolled away from Jesus' tomb and Jesus came back to life.

One of the first times that Jesus was seen again by his friends was when Jesus did another amazing thing...

Jesus' friends were fishing on the lake, but they had caught nothing all night. Early in the morning, they saw a man on the shore.

'Throw your nets on the right side of the boat, and you will catch plenty of fish!' shouted the man.

They did as he told them, and at once their nets were filled with so many fish that they could not pull the nets back into the boat!

Peter, Jesus' dear friend, knew at once that the man on the shore must be Jesus!

He jumped into the water and ran joyfully to Jesus. Jesus was alive again!

John 21, verses 1 to 14

Something to think about:

Peter knew that Jesus was alive because he saw him.

How can we find out more about Jesus?

Prayer:

Dear God, thank you that Jesus is alive and that we can know him too.

Activity:

There are five things wrong with this picture. Can you spot them all?

Published in the UK by
The Bible Reading Fellowship
First Floor, Elsfield Hall, 15-17 Elsfield Way, Oxford OX2 8FG
ISBN 1 84101 408 7

First edition 2004

Editorial Director Annette Reynolds
Art Director Gerald Rogers
Pre-production Krystyna Hewitt
Production John Laister

British Library Cataloguing in Publication Data.
A catalogue record for this book is available from the British Library.

Printed and bound in Singapore